Mr & Mrs

MR & MRS

Summersdale Publishers Ltd
46 West Street
Chichester
West Sussex
PO19 1RP
UK

www.summersdale.com

Printed and bound in China

ISBN: 978-1-84953-891-6

Substantial discounts on bulk quantities of Summersdale books are available to corporations, professional associations and other organisations. For details contact Nicky Douglas by telephone: +44 (0) 1243 756902, fax: +44 (0) 1243 786300 or email: nicky@summersdale.com.

Mr & Mrs

TO..... Fres ....

FROM..... Lynne ....

xxx

WINDSOR 2016

THE HIGHEST HAPPINESS ON EARTH IS MARRIAGE.

- WILLIAM LYON PHELPS -

YOU MAKE MY HEART SKIP A BEAT.

WHAT A HAPPY
and holy fashion
IT IS THAT THOSE
WHO LOVE
one another
SHOULD REST
on the same
pillow.

- Nathaniel Hawthorne -

The Exchange

We pledged our hearts, my love and I,

I in my arms the maiden clasping;

I could not guess the reason why,

But, Oh! I trembled like an aspen.

Her father's love she bade me gain;

I went, but shook like any reed!

I strove to act the man – in vain!

We had exchanged our hearts indeed.

- SAMUEL TAYLOR COLERIDGE -

KEEP YOUR ROMANCE FLOURISHING BY PLACING LOVE NOTES IN THE LEAST EXPECTED PLACES.

"

SUCCESS IN MARRIAGE
DOES NOT COME MERELY
THOUGH FINDING THE
RIGHT MATE, BUT THROUGH
BEING THE RIGHT MATE.

- BARNETT R. BRICKNER -

"

FRIENDSHIP IN MARRIAGE IS THE SPARK THAT LIGHTS AN EVERLASTING FLAME.

- FAWN WEAVER -

BE PATIENT WITH ONE ANOTHER.

There is no such cosy combination as man and wife.

- MENANDER -

A SUCCESSFUL MARRIAGE REQUIRES FALLING IN LOVE MANY TIMES — ALWAYS WITH THE SAME PERSON.

TRUST & BE TRUSTWORTHY.

THE QUIET MUTUAL
gaze of a trusting
HUSBAND AND WIFE
IS LIKE THE FIRST
moment of refuge
FROM A GREAT
weariness or a
great danger.

- GEORGE ELIOT -

Take interest
in each other's
hobbies.

OUR WEDDING DAY
WAS MANY YEARS AGO.
THE CELEBRATION
CONTINUES TO THIS DAY.

- GENE PERRET -

TRUE LOVE
IS THE
JOY OF LIFE.

- JOHN CLARKE -

DREAMS ARE
MADE OF YOU

&

ME.

MARRIAGE:
that I call the
WILL OF TWO TO
CREATE THE ONE
who is more
THAN THOSE
who created it.

- FRIEDRICH NIETZSCHE -

Love
conquers
all.

WHEN I GET MARRIED, I WANT TO BE REALLY MARRIED.

- AUDREY HEPBURN -

TO MY DEAR AND LOVING HUSBAND

If ever two were one, then surely we;

If ever man were lov'd by wife, then thee;

If ever wife was happy in a man,

Compare with me, ye women, if you can.

I prize thy love more than whole mines of gold,

Or all the riches that the East doth hold.

My love is such that rivers cannot quench,

Nor aught but love from thee, give recompence.

Thy love is such I can no way repay;

The heavens reward thee manifold, I pray.

Then while we live in love let's so persever

That when we live no more we may live ever.

- ANNE BRADSTREET -

THE MOST BEAUTIFUL THING TO SEE IS THE PERSON YOU LOVE SMILING.

"

A HAPPY MARRIAGE IS A LONG CONVERSATION,

WHICH ALWAYS SEEMS TOO SHORT. **"**

- ANDRÉ MAUROIS -

WHATEVER OUR SOULS ARE MADE OF, HIS AND MINE ARE THE SAME.

- EMILY BRONTË -

Little acts of love make a big difference.

LOVE DOES NOT consist of gazing **AT EACH OTHER, BUT IN LOOKING** *together in the* **SAME DIRECTION.**

- ANTOINE DE SAINT-EXUPÉRY -

TRUE LOVE IS LOVING SOMEONE FOR WHO THEY ARE.

BETWEEN A MAN AND HIS WIFE NOTHING OUGHT TO RULE BUT LOVE.

- WILLIAM PENN -

ALL YOU NEED
IS LOVE. THE REST
IS JUST ICING ON
THE CAKE.

THERE IS NO MORE
lovely, friendly
AND CHARMING
RELATIONSHIP,
communion or
COMPANY THAN
a good marriage.

- MARTIN LUTHER -

Where there is love there is life.

- MAHATMA GANDHI -

STEP OUTSIDE

&

GAZE
AT THE STARS
TOGETHER.

YOU KNOW YOU'RE IN LOVE
WHEN YOU CAN'T FALL ASLEEP
BECAUSE REALITY IS FINALLY
BETTER THAN YOUR DREAMS.

- ANONYMOUS -

" NOBODY HAS EVER MEASURED, NOT EVEN POETS, HOW MUCH THE HEART CAN HOLD. "

- ZELDA FITZGERALD -

ONLY WE

Dream no more that grief and pain
Could such hearts as ours enchain,
Safe from loss and safe from gain,
Free, as Love makes free.

When false friends pass coldly by,
Sigh, in earnest pity, sigh,
Turning thine unclouded eye
Up from them to me.

Hear not danger's trampling feet
Feel not sorrow's wintry sleet
Trust that life is just and meet,
With mine arm round Thee.

Lip on lip, and eye to eye,
Love to love, we live, we die;
No more Thou, and no more I,
We, and only We!

- RICHARD MONCKTON MILNES HOUGHTON -

MAKE IT A HABIT TO INCLUDE LOVING GESTURES IN YOUR LIFE TOGETHER EVERY DAY, SUCH AS A HUG, A KISS OR A MASSAGE.

BEING DEEPLY LOVED BY SOMEONE GIVES YOU STRENGTH, WHILE LOVING SOMEONE DEEPLY GIVES YOU COURAGE.

- LAO TZU -

IF I HAD A FLOWER
FOR EVERY TIME
I THOUGHT OF YOU...
I COULD WALK THROUGH
MY GARDEN FOREVER.

- ANONYMOUS -

LOVE IS AN ACTION VERB.

We loved with
a love that was
more than love.

- EDGAR ALLAN POE -

WHEN I SAW YOU I FELL IN LOVE, AND YOU SMILED BECAUSE YOU KNEW.

- ARRIGO BOITO -

ASK FRIENDS TO RECOMMEND
THE MOST ROMANTIC
RESTAURANT THEY KNOW

TAKE YOUR PARTNER
THERE FOR A SURPRISE.

"

WHO, BEING LOVED,
IS POOR?

- OSCAR WILDE -

"

ROMANCE

is the glamour

WHICH TURNS

THE DUST

of everyday

LIFE INTO A

golden haze.

- ELINOR GLYN -

HAVE FAITH.
TRUST IS AN IMPORTANT INGREDIENT IN THE RECIPE OF LOVE.

TRUST YOUR HEART IF THE SEAS CATCH FIRE, LIVE BY LOVE THOUGH THE STARS WALK BACKWARD.

- E. E. CUMMINGS -

A happy marriage is the union of two good forgivers.

- RUTH GRAHAM -

APPRECIATE ONE ANOTHER.

GROW OLD ALONG WITH ME!
THE BEST IS YET TO BE.

- ROBERT BROWNING -

COME, LET'S BE A COMFORTABLE COUPLE AND TAKE CARE OF EACH OTHER!

- CHARLES DICKENS -

FROM The Angel in the House

Across the sky the daylight crept,
And birds grew garrulous in the grove,
And on my marriage-morn I slept
A soft sleep, undisturb'd by love.

- COVENTRY PATMORE -

STRONG RELATIONSHIPS ARE BUILT ON FOUNDATIONS OF TRUST & RESPECT.

THE BRIDE AND GROOM -
may their joys
BE AS BRIGHT
AS THE MORNING,
and their sorrows
BUT SHADOWS
that fade in the sunlight
of love.

- MINNA THOMAS ANTRIM -

IN DREAMS AND IN LOVE THERE ARE NO IMPOSSIBILITIES.

- JANOS ARNAY -

EVERY RELATIONSHIP HAS UPS

DOWNS; IT'S HOW YOU RIDE THE WAVES TOGETHER THAT COUNTS.

IN ALL THE WORLD,
there is no
HEART FOR ME
LIKE YOURS.
In all the world,
THERE IS NO LOVE
for you like mine.

- MAYA ANGELOU -

LOVERS DON'T FINALLY MEET SOMEWHERE. THEY'RE IN EACH OTHER ALL ALONG.

- RUMI -

GO ON A DATE
ONCE A WEEK

TAKE IT IN TURNS TO
CHOOSE WHAT YOU DO.

MARRIAGES ARE LIKE FINGERPRINTS; EACH ONE IS DIFFERENT, EACH ONE IS BEAUTIFUL.

- MAGGIE REYES -

LOVE ME WHEN I LEAST DESERVE IT, BECAUSE THAT'S WHEN I REALLY NEED IT.

- SWEDISH PROVERB -

HUGS NOURISH THE SOUL.

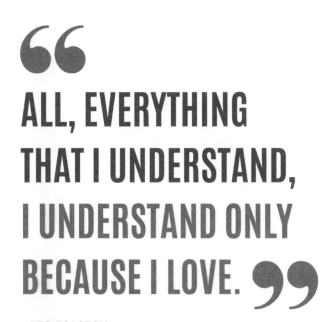

66

ALL, EVERYTHING
THAT I UNDERSTAND,
I UNDERSTAND ONLY
BECAUSE I LOVE. 99

- LEO TOLSTOY -

I FELL IN LOVE
the way you
FALL ASLEEP:
SLOWLY,
and then
ALL AT ONCE.

- JOHN GREEN -

REMINISCE ABOUT YOUR FAVOURITE MEMORIES AS A COUPLE, WHETHER IT'S DATES, HOLIDAYS OR HILARIOUS DISASTERS.

Love is a smoke
raised with the
fume of sighs.

- WILLIAM SHAKESPEARE -

COMING TOGETHER
is a beginning;
KEEPING TOGETHER
IS PROGRESS;
working together
IS SUCCESS.

- HENRY FORD -

Sonnet 116

Let me not to the marriage of true minds
Admit impediments. Love is not love
Which alters when it alteration finds,
Or bends with the remover to remove:
O, no; it is an ever-fixed mark,
That looks on tempests and is never shaken;
It is the star to every wandering bark,
Whose worth's unknown, although his height be taken.
Love's not Time's fool, though rosy lips and cheeks
Within his bending sickle's compass come;
Love alters not with his brief hours and weeks,
But bears it out even to the edge of doom.
If this be error and upon me prov'd,
I never writ, nor no man ever lov'd.

- WILLIAM SHAKESPEARE -

TALKING BRINGS COUPLES CLOSER TOGETHER.

IT WAS ONLY A SUNNY SMILE, AND LITTLE IT COST IN THE GIVING, BUT LIKE MORNING LIGHT IT SCATTERED THE NIGHT AND MADE THE DAY WORTH LIVING.

- F. SCOTT FITZGERALD -

LIFE WITHOUT
love is like
A TREE
WITHOUT
blossoms
OR FRUIT.

- KAHLIL GIBRAN -

COMPLETE EACH OTHER. DON'T COMPETE WITH EACH OTHER.

MARRIAGE, ULTIMATELY, IS THE PRACTICE OF BECOMING PASSIONATE FRIENDS.

- BARBARA DE ANGELIS -

THERE IS NOTHING NOBLER **OR MORE** ADMIRABLE **THAN WHEN** TWO PEOPLE **WHO SEE** EYE TO EYE **KEEP HOUSE AS** MAN AND WIFE.

- HOMER -

DISCUSS YOUR DREAMS FOR THE FUTURE TOGETHER

&

MAKE THEM HAPPEN.

The heart has its reasons which reason knows not.

- BLAISE PASCAL -

Marriage is a mosaic you build with your spouse.

- JENNIFER SMITH -

TAKE A MOMENT TO CONSIDER WHAT YOU CAN DO TO MAKE YOUR SPOUSE'S LIFE BETTER.

LOVE IS COMPOSED OF A SINGLE SOUL INHABITING TWO BODIES.

- ARISTOTLE -

HAPPY MARRIAGES begin when we **MARRY THE ONES** THAT WE LOVE, *and they blossom* **WHEN WE LOVE** the ones we marry.

- TOM MULLEN -

COOK A ROMANTIC MEAL TOGETHER AND DINE BY CANDLELIGHT.

"

TO FIND SOMEONE WHO WILL
LOVE YOU FOR NO REASON,
AND TO SHOWER THAT
PERSON WITH REASONS, THAT
IS THE ULTIMATE HAPPINESS.

- ROBERT BRAULT -

"

For you see,
each day I love
you more.

- ROSEMONDE GÉRARD -

My Wife

Trusty, dusky, vivid, true,
With eyes of gold and bramble-dew,
Steel-true and blade-straight,
The great artificer
Made my mate.

Honour, anger, valour, fire;
A love that life could never tire,
Death quench or evil stir,
The mighty master
Gave to her.

Teacher, tender comrade, wife,
A fellow-farer true through life,
Heart-whole and soul-free
The august father
Gave to me.

- ROBERT LOUIS STEVENSON -

COMPLIMENT YOUR SPOUSE ON SOMETHING DIFFERENT EVERY WEEK.

A HUNDRED HEARTS WOULD BE TOO FEW TO CARRY ALL MY LOVE FOR YOU.

- ANONYMOUS -

True love stories never have endings.

- RICHARD BACH -

EXPLORE A NEW PLACE TOGETHER.

LOVE ISN'T
something
YOU FIND.

LOVE IS

something

THAT FINDS YOU.

- LORETTA YOUNG -

EVER THINE, EVER MINE, EVER OURS.

- LUDWIG VAN BEETHOVEN -

HOLD HANDS MORE, EVEN WHEN YOU'RE WATCHING TELEVISION.

**TWO SOULS BUT WITH
A SINGLE THOUGHT;
TWO HEARTS THAT
BEAT AS ONE.**

- JOHN KEATS -

FOR BEAUTIFUL LIPS, SPEAK
ONLY WORDS OF KINDNESS;
AND FOR POISE, WALK WITH
THE KNOWLEDGE THAT YOU
ARE NEVER ALONE.

- AUDREY HEPBURN -

MAKE YOUR PARTNER
A PACKED LUNCH

SURPRISE THEM
WITH A LOVING
NOTE INSIDE.

Love one another and
you will be happy.

- MICHAEL LEUNIG -

NO JEALOUSY THEIR

dawn of love overcast,

NOR BLASTED WERE

THEIR WEDDED DAYS

with strife; each season

LOOKED DELIGHTFUL

as it past, to the

fond husband and

THE FAITHFUL WIFE.

- JAMES BEATTIE -

MAKING TIME FOR EACH OTHER MATTERS.

"

LIKE GOOD WINE, MARRIAGE
IMPROVES WITH AGE. **"**

- GENE PERRET -

I LOVE YOU FOR ALL
THAT YOU ARE, FOR
ALL YOU HAVE BEEN

FOR ALL YOU
ARE YET TO BE.

A Marriage Ring

The ring, so worn as you behold,

So thin, so pale, is yet of gold:

The passion such it was to prove –

Worn with life's cares, love yet was love.

- GEORGE CRABBE -

SHARED JOY IS DOUBLE JOY; SHARED SORROW IS HALF A SORROW.

- SWEDISH PROVERB -

THE REAL ACT of marriage **TAKES PLACE IN THE HEART,** *not in the* **BALLROOM,** or church, **or synagogue.**

- BARBARA DE ANGELIS -

I LOVE YOU NOT ONLY FOR WHAT YOU ARE BUT FOR WHAT I AM WHEN I AM WITH YOU.

Are we not like two volumes of one book?

- MARCELINE DESBORDES-VALMORE -

❝

NO ROAD IS
LONG WITH
GOOD COMPANY.

- TURKISH PROVERB -

❞

I WANT YOU TODAY,
TOMORROW,
THE NEXT DAY

&

FOR THE
REST OF
MY LIFE.

UNDER EVERY FULL
MOON ARE LOVERS
IN LOVE AND UNDER
EVERY BRIGHT SUN TWO
FRIENDS SMILE AS ONE.

- TERRI GUILLEMETS -

IF YOU LIVE TO
be a hundred,
I WANT TO LIVE TO

BE A HUNDRED

minus one day

SO I NEVER

have to live

without you.

- A. A. MILNE -

BUY EACH OTHER THOUGHTFUL LITTLE GIFTS TO SHOW YOU CARE.

We are shaped
and fashioned by
those we love.

- JOHANN WOLFGANG
VON GOETHE -

FAITH MAKES ALL THINGS POSSIBLE. LOVE MAKES ALL THINGS EASY.

- DWIGHT MOODY -

LOVE IS NOT WHO YOU
CAN SEE YOURSELF WITH.
IT IS WHO YOU CAN'T SEE
YOURSELF WITHOUT.

ONE HALF OF

me is yours,

THE OTHER HALF YOURS,

MINE OWN,

I would say;

BUT IF MINE,

then yours,

And so all yours.

- WILLIAM SHAKESPEARE -

**LEARN TO DO
ALL THE THINGS
THAT MAKE YOUR
SPOUSE FEEL LOVED.**

IT IS NOT A LACK OF LOVE, BUT A LACK OF FRIENDSHIP THAT MAKES UNHAPPY MARRIAGES.

- FRIEDRICH NIETZSCHE -

from Marriage Morning

Light, so low in the vale,
You flash and lighten afar,
For this is the golden morning of love,
And you are his morning star.
Flash, I am coming, I come,
By meadow and stile and wood,
Oh, lighten into my eyes and heart,
Into my heart and my blood!

Heart, are you great enough
For a love that never tires?
O heart, are you great enough for love?
I have heard of thorns and briers.
Over the thorns and briers,
Over the meadows and stiles,
Over the world to the end of it
Flash for a million miles.

- ALFRED, LORD TENNYSON -

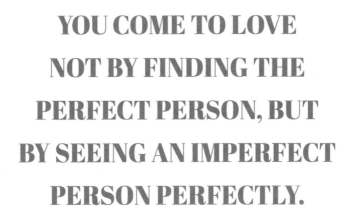

YOU COME TO LOVE
NOT BY FINDING THE
PERFECT PERSON, BUT
BY SEEING AN IMPERFECT
PERSON PERFECTLY.

- SAM KEEN -

DON'T LET DAYS
GO BY WHERE
YOU DON'T SMILE

HUG EACH OTHER.

THE GOAL IN MARRIAGE IS NOT TO THINK ALIKE, BUT TO THINK TOGETHER.

- ROBERT C. DODDS -

EVERY SO OFTEN,
REMEMBER TO TURN OFF
THE TELEVISION, CUDDLE
UP ON THE SOFA

&

TALK.

WHEN WE GOT MARRIED I TOLD MY WIFE, 'IF YOU LEAVE ME, I'M GOING WITH YOU.' AND SHE NEVER DID.

- JAMES McBRIDE -

MAKE TIME FOR INTIMACY.

WHAT I LOVE MOST ABOUT MY HOME IS WHO I SHARE IT WITH.

- TAD CARPENTER -

YOU ARE
the butter
TO MY BREAD,
AND THE BREATH
to my life.

- JULIA CHILD -

PHONE EACH OTHER OFTEN,
EVEN IF IT IS FOR NO
PARTICULAR REASON
OTHER THAN TO SAY,
'I LOVE YOU.'

WEDDINGS TO ME ARE WONDROUS BECAUSE THEY ARE SO FILLED WITH TOMORROWS.

- MARY FORSELL -

TAKE SOME TIME
OFF WORK

&

PLAN A ROMANTIC
GETAWAY.

HAVING A PLACE
to go is home.
HAVING SOMEONE
TO LOVE
is family.
HAVING BOTH
is a blessing.

- DONNA HEDGES -

"

THE FIRST THING I DID WHEN I SOLD MY BOOK WAS TO BUY A NEW WEDDING RING FOR MY WIFE AND ASK HER TO MARRY ME ALL OVER AGAIN.

- NICHOLAS SPARKS -

FALL IN LOVE WITH ONE ANOTHER MORE THAN ONCE.

Marriage is the perfection which love aimed at.

- RALPH WALDO EMERSON -

SONNETS FROM THE PORTUGUESE XLIII

How do I love thee? Let me count the ways.
I love thee to the depth and breadth and height
My soul can reach, when feeling out of sight
For the ends of Being and ideal Grace.
I love thee to the level of everyday's
Most quiet need, by sun and candle-light.
I love thee freely, as men strive for Right;
I love thee purely, as they turn from Praise.
I love thee with the passion put to use
In my old griefs, and with my childhood's faith.
I love thee with a love I seemed to lose
With my lost saints, – I love thee with the breath,
Smiles, tears, of all my life! – and, if God choose,
I shall but love thee better after death.

- ELIZABETH BARRETT BROWNING -

NEVER FORGET YOU ARE PART OF A TEAM; YOU ARE ON THE SAME SIDE!

MY MOST
brilliant
ACHIEVEMENT

WAS MY ABILITY TO

PERSUADE
my love to

marry me.

- WINSTON CHURCHILL -

"

HAVE A HEART THAT NEVER HARDENS, AND A TEMPER THAT NEVER TIRES, AND A TOUCH THAT NEVER HURTS.

- CHARLES DICKENS -

LOVE WITH YOUR HEART.

You have my whole heart for my whole life.

- FRENCH PROVERB -

IN ALL OF THE
WEDDING CAKE, HOPE IS
THE SWEETEST OF PLUMS.

- DOUGLAS JERROLD -

TAKE TIME TO
SNUGGLE WITH YOUR
PARTNER BEFORE
GOING TO SLEEP

GETTING UP IN
THE MORNING.

NOW JOIN YOUR HANDS, AND WITH YOUR HANDS YOUR HEARTS.

- WILLIAM SHAKESPEARE -

MAKE EACH OTHER LAUGH.

WE LOVE BECAUSE IT'S THE ONLY TRUE ADVENTURE.

- NIKKI GIOVANNI -

Marriages are made in heaven.

- ENGLISH PROVERB -

SHARE
everything
WITH EACH OTHER.
EXPRESSING
the way you feel
IS IMPORTANT.

LOVE IS SMILING ON THE INSIDE AND OUT.

- JENNIFER WILLIAMS -

MARRIAGE IS THE AGREEMENT TO LET A FAMILY HAPPEN.

- BETTIE JANE WYLIE -

Love's Philosophy

The fountains mingle with the river
And the rivers with the Ocean,
The winds of Heaven mix for ever
With a sweet emotion;
Nothing in the world is single;
All things by a law divine
In one spirit meet and mingle.
Why not I with thine?
See the mountains kiss high Heaven
And the waves clasp one another;
No sister-flower would be forgiven
If it disdained its brother;
And the sunlight clasps the earth
And the moonbeams kiss the sea:
What is all this sweet work worth
If thou kiss not me?

- PERCY BYSSHE SHELLEY -

WEDDINGS ARE NOT OVER UNTIL THEY ARE SEALED WITH A KISS.

- SUSAN MARG -

"

NEVER MARRY FOR LOVE;
BUT SEE THAT THOU LOV'ST
WHAT IS LOVELY. **"**

- WILLIAM PENN -

WHEN I'M WITH YOU, NOTHING ELSE MATTERS.

Marriage follows on love as smoke on flame.

- NICOLAS CHAMFORT -

66

LOVE IS A SYMBOL OF ETERNITY. **99**

- GERMAINE DE STAËL -

DON'T TAKE each other **FOR GRANTED.** YOU HAVE TO *work at it* ALL THE TIME.

AND WHEN LOVE SPEAKS,
THE VOICE OF ALL THE GODS
MAKES HEAVEN DROWSY
WITH THE HARMONY.

- WILLIAM SHAKESPEARE -

TO GET THE FULL VALUE OF A JOY YOU MUST HAVE SOMEONE TO DIVIDE IT WITH.

- MARK TWAIN -

RENEW YOUR LOVE FOR EACH OTHER EVERY DAY.

If you're interested in finding out more about our books,
find us on Facebook at **Summersdale Publishers** and
follow us on Twitter at **@Summersdale**.

www.summersdale.com